Mary Kom
The Boxer

Written by
Kunal Kapsime

Illustrated by
Luiz Malon

This is the story of grit and determination of Mary Kom, a boxer who overcame all odds to become a world champion.

Mary was born in a rural area in Manipur, a state in the North-Eastern part of India in 1982. She lived with her parents, a younger brother and a sister.

Things were difficult for her family, as her parents were farmers, and they struggled to make ends meet. As a little girl, she helped them on the farm and also took care of her younger siblings. At a very young age, she learned to be responsible and hard-working.

Mary's father was a wrestler in his younger days and he encouraged her to participate in sports at school. Mary took a keen interest in sports and excelled at football, volleyball and athletics. However, she had never done boxing.

In 1998, Dingko Singh, a boxer from Mary' home state of Manipur won the gold medal at the Asian games. His success inspired Mary to try boxing, and very soon it became her passion.

But pursuing boxing was a distant dream for Mary, because in those days it was not considered a sport intended for women. Even Mary's parents did not encourage her to participate in boxing.

Mary knew that the road ahead was going to be difficult, but she was determined to follow her dreams. She decided to leave her hometown to join a Sports Academy located in a big city. There, she started training for boxing with a coach.

Mary was a quick learner, and after just six months of training she won the state boxing championship. Her first win gave her a lot of confidence and she saw it as a chance to advance her boxing career. Her success also convinced her parents of her potential in boxing, and they started supporting her.

Mary's first international medal came the following year in USA, where she won the silver medal in Women's World Boxing Championship.
But, she lost the final match to another boxer who was more experienced than her.

However, she did not give up on her dream of winning the world championship. She trained very hard and won the gold medal at the next year's event held in Turkey. This marked the beginning of Mary's incredible journey in this sport. Over the next few years, she won the Women's world boxing championship six times.

Her most important win came in 2012, when Mary made history by becoming the first woman from India to win a bronze medal in boxing at the London Olympics. Her entire country was very proud of her.

She also became the first Indian woman to win a gold medal in boxing at the Asian games in 2014 in Incheon, Korea.

For her achievements, Mary was honored by several national awards and recognitions in India, including the Padma Vibhushan award which is the second-highest civilian award in India. She was also nominated as a Member of Parliament by the President of India.

With her courage and willpower, Mary was able to overcome many difficulties and follow her dreams. "Don't give up, as there is always a next time", she said. Her story continues to inspire the next generation of girls to not give up on their dreams.